6 Apply force and press down on the string. This should be more secure.

7 Keep pressing down. See how much force the string can hold.

Principle at Play

This model shows how a real suspension bridge works. Bridges need a lot of support. The book stacks anchored the string and stabilized the standing books. The standing books are like towers. Keep experimenting. Change the size of the books. Use different strings. Test the strength and stability.

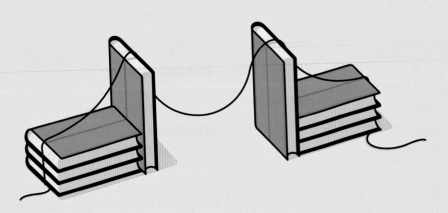

Pebble® Plus

Monkeys
Spider Monkeys

by Mary R. Dunn

Consulting Editor: Gail Saunders-Smith, PhD

Consultant: Lori Perkins,
Vice President of Collections
Zoo Atlanta, Atlanta, Georgia

CAPSTONE PRESS
a capstone imprint

Pebble Plus is published by Capstone Press,
1710 Roe Crest Drive, North Mankato, Minnesota 56003
www.capstonepub.com

Library of Congress Cataloging-in-Publication Data
Cataloging-in-publication information is on file with the Library of Congress.
ISBN 978-1-62065-104-9 (library binding)
ISBN 978-1-4765-1082-8 (ebook PDF)

Editorial Credits
Christopher L. Harbo, editor; Bobbie Nuytten, designer; Svetlana Zhurkin, media researcher;
Eric Manske, production specialist

Photo Credits
Alamy: Bryan Lowry, 5; Biosphoto: Cyril Ruoso, 17; Getty Images: David Tipling, 13; iStockphotos: Devon Stephens, cover;
Minden Pictures: Pete Oxford, 11; Newscom: Danita Delimont Photography/Jim Goldstein, 19, Image Broker/jspix, 7, 9;
Shutterstock: Graham Prentice, 1, 15, Jamie Robinson, 21

Note to Parents and Teachers

The Monkeys set supports national science standards related to life science. This book describes and illustrates spider monkeys. The images support early readers in understanding the text. The repetition of words and phrases helps early readers learn new words. This book also introduces early readers to subject-specific vocabulary words, which are defined in the Glossary section. Early readers may need assistance to read some words and to use the Table of Contents, Glossary, Read More, Internet Sites, and Index sections of the book.

Printed in the United States of America in North Mankato, Minnesota.
092012   006933CGS13

Table of Contents

Treetop Tumblers

A small brown monkey hangs

from a tree branch by its tail.

It dangles like a spider.

No wonder it's called

a spider monkey.

Seven kinds of spider monkeys
live in Mexico, Central America,
and South America.
They make their homes
high in the trees.

where spider monkeys live

6

Up Close

Spider monkeys have gray,

brown, red, tan, or black coats.

Some have white rings

around their eyes.

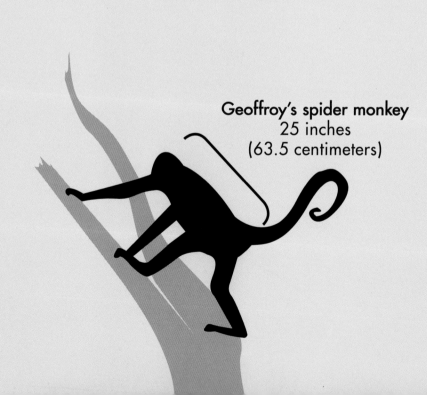

Geoffroy's spider monkey
25 inches
(63.5 centimeters)

6 feet
(183 cm)

Spider monkeys' legs
and tails are very long.
They use their strong tails
like an extra hand.

Finding Food

In small groups, spider monkeys look for food. Their favorite food is fruit. They also munch on leaves, flowers, and insects.

Growing Up

Female spider monkeys have

one baby every four to five years.

Baby spider monkeys have pink

rings of skin around their eyes.

Baby spider monkeys
stay with their mothers
for about four years.
Spider monkeys live
about 27 years in the wild.

Keeping Safe

Large cats such as jaguars and

pumas hunt spider monkeys.

When they sense danger,

spider monkeys shout.

They also shake tree branches.

Spider monkeys lose
their forest homes when
people cut down trees.
Most spider monkeys
are now endangered.

21

Glossary

coat—an animal's hair or fur

dangle—to swing or hang down loosely

endangered—in danger of dying out

favorite—a thing or person that you like best

sense—to feel or be aware of your surroundings

Read More

Gosman, Gillian. *Spider Monkeys*. Monkey Business. New York: PowerKids Press, 2012.

Jordan, Apple. *Guess Who Grabs*. Guess Who. New York: Marshall Cavendish Benchmark, 2012.

Riggs, Kate. *Monkeys*. Seedlings. Mankato, Minn.: Creative Education, 2012.

Internet Sites

FactHound offers a safe, fun way to find Internet sites related to this book. All of the sites on FactHound have been researched by our staff.

Here's all you do:

Visit *www.facthound.com*

Type in this code: 9781620651049

Super-cool stuff! Check out projects, games and lots more at **www.capstonekids.com**

Index

Word Count: 182
Grade: 1
Early-Intervention Level: 15